MAAfA

Cover design by Eric Amling
Book design by Rebecca Wolff

Published in the United States by

Fence Books
110 Union Street
Second Floor
Hudson NY 12534

www.fenceportal.org

This book was printed by Versa Press
and distributed by Small Press Distribution
and Consortium Book Sales and Distribution.

Library of Congress Cataloguing in Publication Data
Holiday, Harmony [1982–]
Maafa / Harmony Holiday

Library of Congress Control Number: 2021948254
ISBN 13: 978-1-944380-23-6

First Edition
10 9 8 7 6 5 4 3 2

MAAfA

HARMONY HOLIDAY

FENCE BOOKS   Hudson NY

Contents

Preface (to a neverending genocide note)

SAY HER NAME

Inspection / at auction   1

Maafa's tongue is in   the world's mouth (annihilation)   3

Little bits of ride breaking with the assembly line I   5

Go forth and tell no one   6

Mitochondria   7

Tragic Cities   8

Looting / Illusion   10

Maafa's Babygirl   11

Maafa's Moments of Revelation   12

Maafa's   Narratives of Progress   15

Motherless Empire   17

DUAT

Duat   21

God Bless the Child   26

Disinherited Trauma   27

Kafka on the Slaveship   28

Monsters   of Innocence   29

Maafa, Maybe   30

Far Beyond Hysteria   31

Headless Heroes   32

Laugh, Clown, Laugh   34

In Praise of New Beginnings   35

Man, God Ain't Like That   36

Ma Leaving   37

Ma's Restorative Gasping   38

The alienation of labor is almost complete.   40

The Damned/Don't   Cry   42

Yeah ! / Compulsion to Inherit the Wind   44

Black Anguish   45

Duat   46

Escape Scene   48

Leaving Duat/Got Til it's Gone   49

Leitmotif (*Run*)

My Danger   as   Her   51

Maafa's   Toneburst   52

No Discernable Radical Politics, *Run*   54

Pact   55

Maafa Knows Benthos   56

Settlers, *Run*   57

Ma's   Occasional Dancing Objects   59

Who is you?   60

Genocide, Patricide,   Ma's   alive   61

Maafa's   Kef   62

Where do you stay?   64

Maafa   22   65

Maafa in Constant Gardens   66

Vicious Nonchalance   67

Maafa 11   68

Ravishments   69

Dusk, Ma   70

Ma's Favorite   71

Maafa's Waist-Length   74

Militancy / Intimacy   75

A PARADISE OF RUINS

Not that we begged to be stolen or still mistake a killer for a chaperone   81

A Tangle of Pathology   84

Here is a southern   gothic tale   that's   true   89

Tender Disintegration   104

Preface (to a neverending genocide note)

Maafa ██
██ Maafa, ██████████████████
██ Maafa, █████████████
██
██
██ *Maafa*, haaaaa, gotcha, awful-ma, father, *ma ah fuh*—haggle and hobble of vowels, quiteloud echo of mother and father and less and excess and access and after and before and awful and fault and falling and fuck ah fuck, the other, the fuzzy elsewhere: *Maafa* with a gust of captive beauty, muted tunnel under itself, sense of ruin upheld by a future, performance of what is not but nothing but the black future. Sham and shambled and ours. Maafa ██
██
█████████████████████████████ Maafa ███
██
████████████████████████████ Maafa is our arrow/route into the incessant ███████
████████████████████████████████████ shape-shifting from idea to woman. An exalted exile ████████
███

██████████████ Maafa ███
██
███████████████████████████████████████ Maafa is a girl, a woman, a black divinity and epic hero(ine) who, in learning her name for the first time, remembers ████████████
████████ She is also a killer, ██
██████████ trickster, a priest, a greedy unintelligibility and selfless coherence. She is a girl who witnessed the massacre of her own family and forgot until now, blames herself, wonders if she did it herself even though she knows who ██████ and holds the culprits in her mind like shocks and rivets and never recovered bodies that ache in their blankness. █████
██
██
███ Look at Maafa. Look at god.

This is the story of a woman who has witnessed the massacre of her own family

A disaster is no respecter of   mirrors
Do we have any black women in the epic hero position?
Any black witness?

SAY HER NAME

Inspection / at auction

Breasts   full   middled

Face   radiant   comfort girl or inhouse breeder

Equipment   ripe   unreconciled   no prior attempts

Stance   bitter   ravenous   recoiled

Hate makes her servile

Buttocks   firm   raised   wide

Hiding style   plain sight

Petite frame   tribal marking on the face above right upper lip   entropic indent

Mouth   full/careful

Teeth   so hip   made to break the language open & fix her name a home

Likelihood of inducing owner's empathy   or love   or lust   high

Likelihood she has suitors of her own kind   certain

Likelihood they will take the whip for her or run away when held at gunpoint   unclear

Likelihood the president will date her on stage   unknown, what are you even saying?

Name : M a a f a

Meaning   Black Holocaust   astonishing surrender   ma at   kick rocks, those are diamonds

Beautiful walking graves chased off the water

Skin   perfect no blemishes or permutations in pigment

Hair   coiled   star in the center of a tight afro   scar of a star

Eyes   unimpressed   still a little wistful

Nose   wide & aquiline at the same time

Symmetry   impeccable   dangerous

Tone of voice   bewildered

Likelihood she'd call Jesus daddy?

(No father figures, hear?)

Maafa's tongue is in   the world's mouth   (annihilation)

This is the story of a woman who has witnessed   the massacre of her own family   and cannot tell
if she was helpful in committing   if she committed if she is always committing   the crimes she is
witnessing   if the commitment to witnessing is a commitment to crime   She watched them and held
onto the memory of their killers so hard she cannot remember if they were her or hers
belonging to her commitment to seeing them   invited like company   and she their hired black
witness   She cannot remember   what she is committed to   understanding

3

Maafa how we spun in the sunny under   standing (outlived slander & the ban on perms)

Looking   for   a place to keep your memories   like a body or belief system

And each one we   found   we destroyed   those women

4

Little bits of ride breaking with the assembly line *I*

Not that we begged to be stolen or mistook our killers for chaperones but I

wanted the one who made a razor out of his shackles and carved stars into all our skulls

I dream of that neurotic negus Van Gogh

so good with his hands he cuts them off like wrong answers on a work song's bent wing

It's getting cool to lose our minds   Insanity is an ambition here   like   doctor lawyer crazy nigger

A professional class   flatters the captors

spend our time in danger desiring shovels and pebbles for singers

In Mississippi he asked me could I kill him and leave him with Ruth by the river

Ever wonder who taught you that need is dirty?

You be the backwoods ruby mangling the new black fist into televisions who taught you dirty needing, some kinesis

this built-in longing for what oppresses

Filthy cargo   there he goes   ashamed of being ready or needy   needle elbow neatness

We're crazy about his tough sweet sound

Go forth and tell no one

Mandarin oranges straight from the can   pinched like pimp hand zeros (heroes?)
I was choking
So I ate only soft things   no chewing   choking on the softening seed of a loose bullet   impaling me
from my mother's throat   Maafa   can't breathe   the boat to shore
Maafa don't study war   no more   or crosshairs or   sparingly
Sometimes we call this *intention*   but in her case   it's that she's onto the banality of horror
She's bored with the angry men   their broken livers bending the skin between the brows
    Into   ladders   and venture capital
This is   the   end   of   the beginning of   genocide   it begins swallowing soft things
then pans   to Quincy   a   recorder   Edward Kennedy Ellington's steeple chasing him
in   tented Italian   footage of everything but the passage down the canal to level   where
he   calls for notes *no   more innuendo   tell me*

Black beauty is the most powerful currency in the world

Mitochondria

Imma name my baby such. Fuck your lazy syllables. Might 'o con dreamed up a praise name. You know you ghetto if— and I love it. Dictionary claims it's the way we became human, the jaded program windows' automatic roll-up, the soda on the side type DNA lesson made fun on the block in the sun with the double dutch champion and the four wheels on wide feet hunting for fat ass that knows how to leap that rope a joyful scuffle that almost sounds like the sea having been broken but it's just sugar and carbon stuffed in aluminum burning your teeth numb and fast twitch muscles saying higher nigga   it's Sunday   call on the numberless threads of your one mazed identity and swallow them whole bent dial tones then call my baby, flying

Tragic Cities

Her double vowel allows you to moan   in pace with the everyday   arrow   and   hug Willis' huge knuckled
eyes

There she goes!

Sometimes I confuse Jamestown, the place where slaves were docked and traded, naked and inspected, flesh flung
from yes and no, with Jonestown, the cult made up of a bunch of brainwashed lunatics who took their own lives in the
name of desire

                              This world is full of magic cities

Maafa   smirks   to herself   grotesque interiority   always ready to grid and flee

She fled after witnessing the massacre of her own   finally   wasn't sorry   left the bodies to decay and fester

that they   may become her   fertile land

8

Had you call me   *M a a f a*   after the rock cry out. No longer wanna lick you off the sides of my mouth and spit you out in rhymes. Would rather murder you and do my time in doula numerals. I counted tunnels in the funny junkyard, counted the minutes I could spend in open air and forced myself illiterate in maritime values and it was lit
Neurotic with hip teeth and a Thad Jones lisp   We needed to get outside Even if we had we to run up on a liquor store promising *I ain't never coming home no more*   Slow athens   scooting   into   the   voice   of   its enemy to seize some done-already   &   strangle pleas   as your silly   happiness   abdicates   the garden of   my heart   now   she's   black and bleak

Antonia Antigone your   koan   a keeping sphere or   natal   occlusion of country   I   get her off on a technicality   her   name   in   paper and   ash   her *ah* slashing in a mouth of   basket fuzz her choke mufflng   her *Ma a‾fa*   Not   that   she has   forgotten   her   given paper   name   but that   no   one walks it   lovingly to   the   guillotine   nobody   chooses   a   side of her to   mean victim or matriach   hero   or   villain mother   or invisible man & her each scam nonbinary topples   in   the unspoken holocaust of   herself until she is so   human crawling   on   all fours in a   white gown in your   field   muttering about   gone

Looting / Illusion

Like someone who can hear into someone else's hearing   not a spy but captive   clairaudient binge listener

We all fake our deaths with her now   how about that boat cult   pyramid drifting off its fix into forever

Maafa wants us to learn her name before she leaps

She has ignored the massacre of her known family   gleefully   (of archeology, of no bodies or steep evidence
but soft atlantic rage

Blames herself for their fate   is   that vain

and then one day   isn't   hums   *I Should Care*   finds spite where the terror was   and   prayers for Malcolm

whose corpse smiles at her   from the ocean's spurting   stutter   mutters   *Hallelujah*

10

Maafa's Babygirl

In the hollow fuse of doomed adventure M a a f a   got fertile as a flickering November field   and egalitarian indicating rape   or surrender. Middle hysterias mistaken for surrender include   sleep love hunger prayer penetration shredded carrots encased in plastic like descheduled devils' horns   empty FEMA caskets buried deep in the shackled imagination and the placating play cousins whose agape gazes lose track of those playing dead or replace them studiously. Don't ask her meaning, ask her use. I think she had a body or two inside of her when the third one came alive. I know possession works both ways. I've known rivals and they perished trying. I know the canoe sinking into the lake hurls debris at the psyche of each silent threat and the cloying barracudas don't settle in no coy truce like two cars and four walls and emancipation paper ransom note: pagan, pilgrim, roll up   glock in hand and switchbladed bible sandwich. I know when he called me *babygirl* a pressure gathered in my chest, a disgusted readiness disguised as pleasure-seeking, a tribal worm writhing from his heart to mine   and no minor island remedy could be so ready as the womb— Babygirl what's a barracoon?   What's between a miracle and a nightmare? Whiteness ? Where? Yeah, baby, right there, split it open— Maafa finna go in on these wings

Maafa's Moments of Revelation

Rub the mirror with such cotton   it grabs your face like cave light   grins

This gringo family is naive   they let me clean their looking glass

I place an army of wooden dreams where the medicine once lasted for years in variations of pale aggression

It's fun flushing the white pills: maelstrom

It's fun touching the crushed *what if*

diverted to see something spinning in the middle sea like we and coming out alive sedated by praise
like   this

House full of fools letting the slave peer into its drift   glass   It's fun to taste castaway salt on my
gums   maroon gums   swollen ballooning lunatic happiness inside   two illusions

This is also a story about the benefits of losing one's mind in the middle of a violent succession of events Maafa got into this woman Maafa occupied the most receptive and regenerative energy she could find and Maafa took it like bait like aim like fallen fruit like nonlinear radiance taken to entrances like near perfection the flaws become more obvious

Catatonia, my   tongue   is slipping   down   my throat as   the   serpent   lips   my   spine

which is stippled   too   into   the new arrowroute   green   note   la luta   intoned & coaxed honor

bending in every   endlessly sturdy austerity ecstatic   *(you won't need   those chains)*

speechlessness   the place where   thought collects as hive   and   hides   effort in the
                                                                                    force of grace

Swaying so   not yet saying   no   same as saying nothing   Maafa a   muse   in her

atavistic visceral   hold up   that's the girl's   name   a   silent   killing some strange voyeur

yearning   for herself who she is strangling

14

Maafa's Narratives of Progress

I thought it would be   a   moaning place   not   a   screaming place   an alimony to suffer

forward   leave   the mother in her   shambles of   joes and bills   her lilting   green   going

 Now I don't see much difference between ownership and   hysteria   even when all you own

is the   narrative and its never-telling   holding on to this   unconfessed torment like a secret love

   of ruin   and bringing it to life   endlessly   as a private need for ruin   not to punish

but to begin again   to   haunt with renewal   *It's a pleasure to meet you in your visible world*

I haven't met any selfish, intelligent, mentally liberated, and aggressive women before now, before you

Meant as a compliment   Turned her   drooping pentagram into a plan   Not   that   we hadn't

planned to leave before

So   warm   and so vivid -invaded   inflicted   inflected   with nevers

Her firmament   her   cresent edge   readied like   vowels   in   solitude

A   whole   holocaust   *no respector of mirrors* ?

And in that brutalized shy shy earth where whatever you look into like gazing or searching becomes you some clone with your permission of course the looking in their direction for a response is your permission

a lot of children kill our fathers looking into them

Motherless Empire

These are my obsessions   seduced into a second childhood

      Not because I want to correct   something but because   Bess is more seductive as a runner than a
whore   a praise dance like the ones we did in the mirror   with Aunt Viv

Nothing referential the second time around   no referees from commercial enterprise   nothing but
the soil   the crop   the house   their bodies   her second skin   Phallic hypocrisy

Our   sweet babygirl   looking   for reflective water   in the fraying dust

Sometimes I feel that way   and am that way   one piece of cloth for every piece of cloth I   weave and bleach

into   statement   in the sun and stain   in the circus juice of berries

Everything that is mine this time   I am making   Rebirth can only come of this desire to take

what's   yours and embroider it in the code of first witness   This is my godless land   my country my

obsessive fantasy about the corner of a missing smile found in the owl's eyes smirking

calling the mouth a liability   cracking the night with blurry accusations

Weeping out of pity for the devil until   what was convulsive split to slow moan boat song

Song of the recovered darkness

Song of how we longed for that dayless day in secret

Song of how we killed it in a public square while its soul ran off into the eagle, heretic

There is a power that only silence chases in a language of pure gesture between dance and birth

and no nation can claim it   &   have you been   the unmothered skin of early sky

in bondage   bound to   a land as you torched it

DUAT

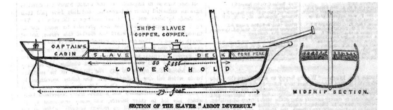

SHIPS SLAVES
COPPER. COPPER.

CAPTAIN'S CABIN | SLAVE | DECK | FORE PEAK
50 feet
LOWER HOLD
79 feet

SECTION OF THE SLAVER "ABBOT DEVEREUX."

MIDSHIP SECTION.

Duat

In Kemetic mythology, the underworld is the interval between day and night, repeating as often as there are days and nights. It's a part of life, you die and resurrect as the sun does. Ra, the sun god is always battling for re-emergence into the mundane world, always fighting with the serpent god of chaos for reentry, an accurate depiction of the habitual emergency that this planet is becoming, and will we eat the sun? Will we cannibalize our own lifeforce? Should we let the serpent win to call its bluff and will our hearts weigh more than a feather at the end of dayless day and be condemned to eternal suffering for being so heavy— be heathen, go heaving, no heaven? Can we surrender personal will to divine will, the source of divinity being the life-giving fire disk in the sky? Can we get back to worshiping life and not death?

The diagrams depicting this underworld could be mistaken for diagrams of the holds of slave ships. The intellectual reflex that lets us all resist prophecy as mystical bs, or the spirit's wishful impressions of its future, also prevents us from understanding every moment's interdependence. *Duat* and *Maafa* or the African Holocaust, are the same event. Duat translates to *other world*, and Maafa is from somewhere else— here and there and underneath and eating the serpent to appease the sun and moving forward toward our myth.

Someday, some daaayyyyyah   somedayyyI I will wear the starry crown   Maafa reminds us

A myth gives us tools to comprehend the archetypal energy animating our realm. Duat and Maafa are one interminable event, a crisis family linked in perpetual death and rebirth until they turn their fate around. The West is that underworld, that chaos, hostile to good destiny— that land of cannibals and madmen we enter to unravel.

Not that I have condoned the theft of my body in order to resurrect an enemy sun

Not that I have been stolen
Not that I am coming forth by day
Not that Maafa got me for a name

Maaaaa fah   I'm speaking again

Not that I'm in the starry crown

It's heavy   it's   attracting thieves

Not that I wanna talk about them

Not that they are the thieves
Not that they are men

Not that anybody can see nobody   can   see

Not that we thought about leisure as a way of looking (see ming) Mingus, I love you

   Not that we   even had a word for it   to give it form

Not that struggle became   a   home   a form   we   could trust

And ease   an evil   an enemy   prickly   unknown   unknowable then

Not that it was riveting to have one enemy with   no   name   no passion but freedom (run) (rain some/ransom)

   Not that they were so free   they believed in nothing

so   they're teaching them to work with their hands and the whole motion of the figure is torment

Not that torment as   a gesture is a black   man laughing in   rehearsal   for the minstrel

What happened between her and the angel that made her change her name? (*I told Jesus*)

   pink satin   helpless response to a miracle

Not that   I am   interrogating   the sun and   pretending to   save it

Maafa   of the criminalized   sun   on Sunday we go wonder about her   in a humble   room
          and   dance   the blank   beat   forward

Not that I feel futile   or was it servile   evil   as a ghost   of the future

My perception   my delusion   my way of naming the labor of their total availability/vitality

A deity is a personification of a spiritual power   and deities who have not been recognized become demons, become
dangerous

Maafa   god of wished-for danger   of excuses   of range   day in   her night   in   her

Not that the   healer   needs   an image   or publicity .   or cohesion

Not   the massacre   becoming   imaginary   camaraderie

To   have   witnessed   the massacre of our own families   nobody   recovers these

No!   nor that

We certainly laugh   a lot   at our   own

                              witnessing   at being owned   property of

To keep from   (like hostages are kept, not like brides or blacks are kept)   crying   somebody weep

Not that it isn't busy happening   guzzling   the sound of our mirth   for   adventure   is
what   she   calls *lil' **inherited trauma*** renters inertia   when   struggle gets boring   and   her
name   ornamental   Ma   my mouth   can't turn   her   into   mirrors

Not   that you can attack   a   disaster   she will   turn into   a city   here an underworld
 gone over
over

God Bless the Child

In the legends they call it *the boat that carries the sun*. I'm staring at a photo of their version of hell, or daybreak, and at another photograph of the hold of a slaveship, when it occurs to me that maybe they're the exact same place and we're the glorying pawns in a centuries-long ritual to get off that boat— sunslaves worshipers holy ripple had our fill, sent to raise the dead to break the day like bread like flesh like sever as a favor, favored, shed. There is no other ruler or under to adore the spun up noose knot didn't wanna use the *n* word of keep goose-stepping toward the guillotine but in looting the underworld for diagrams of tomorrow if you don't go crazy you might go home be named an intruder and killed on the spot, eaten alive.

So let me get this straight: uncoil the Maafa from her root and oceanic brutality there you go again Each night we get on a ship, the subconscious (the body is the subconscious, stay inside it) so we get on this vessel, and on is to in as, back inside of ourselves as this ship, yes. Yes, like cargo. Yes, like this. Follow me. And we navigate a bunch of demons, our own, and if we make it beyond them, like in *Orfeu Negro*, the sun rises. Up, higher! We are like that gleeful child plucking at her own strings until they succumb to their light source. Except for a while we got trapped mid-ritual, victims of our own myth-hoax, kept on the boat, hidden from the sun. We who were sent into bondage to heal the sun having lost track of the purpose of our nightmare and turned it into beautiful music, strengthening it, beating it into our bodies, *Duat, do-aht*, also appears as *tuat, tu-aht, tuer, tyrant* truant way to the sun. How the French say *to kill* we say, *it is risen*, it is returning. We are carrying the sun back to ourselves, as ourselves, such bounty and redundant glory. Maafa on her duat, doo-wop, that thing, that thing. Sun Ra said *god is more than love can ever be* and she wept and watched, **not to be unified with the sun god, but to be judged**. Woke up on the floor covered in butter and feathers, no grudge. Not to be judged, but to be screened, to be such an obedient disaster, such a trusted genocide, such a happy witness to the massacre of sunny side, set aside, sifted. This is the story of a girl who is witnessing the massacre of her own kinship, big ship, with a big myth and a digging name

Disinherited Trauma

What filthy   brittle glee of   misrecognition   releasing its object   that almost filial   will   to   be

Undermined   by   pain   with   nowhere   left   to   travel   but   Solomon   and limp

buttered   teardrop   as   it   slips   from   the   lazy   eyed   window   of   recovery

Now the grand posture is voluntary   not a   petty   strut, a   perfect   strut   revel and ever

So much repeated early   childhood   go ahead   lick the sky   to   see if it's   glass or geese,

for me   for the   humility of tongues when they show   vulgar and slum   when   they shove themselves

into   fresh   snow   thinking   *this   will allow me to   speak picturesquely   about   loss as if I grew up*

on horseback, as if I was born   cold   or

Film sealed too long in a dark box whines like a restless animal

Tongue pressed too long to the roof of an empty house   will make   good kindling

Good kids   good   thatch   good black radical   they'll pet my   head   & only want me

        dead   once   in a while

Distress: this sleek humility of growing out of rage

Kafka on the Slaveship

Nigga what? You thought you could write a hood classic about turning black and free and apathetic and neurotic and narcotic and nilotic   and bloodclot and bumbaclot and working class and shiftless and Peter Tosh and *Lonely Sky Boat* wasn't gonna implode through drafty speakers in the rafters in   the netting in the knee cushions, 'cause we're smugglers too   in ways you wouldn't   suspect or abuse us out of   you   thought   you could wear blackface and lament some baffled magic and   we wouldn't be on the other end of your   victim story   to show you a hoe in the field?

Monsters   of Innocence

She has his statues   stacked flat on their   backs in   the coffin warehouse a   pout of serial numbers and
glaucoma   at   least   that's   what   he tells   mama while lighting   the next blunt   and humming   some soul

Survival was so funny   and incantatory

two   astronaut statues pressed to   my   ears   while I   sing   Malcolm's   valentine

Maafa, Maybe

Samsara   some   arson   pale lace pasties   a legend   a lady of the lungless hills   who licks   their
smokelips   and knows   the   coming   days   Ma a fa   maybe   your   patience is   a   crisis   maybe
your   beauty   curses   the   west   maybe   your   daddy   left   and   mom   is   drunk on   the one   good   rug
and   you're   running   laps   around   her   teasing   the   collapse   of   their   society   to   champion   the   rise
of   your   own   Let   that   be   enough   to   hold   enough roving   accountability   for   one   neverending
black   spring

Him just spray-painting the Mona Lisa, and whatever, with his goons. It is really the most satisfying thing you could
do, is to just put a little scratch in something that thinks it — that has the arrogance of knowing what it is

Not that Maafa   committed   patricide
   Our   maiden   is   guiltless   wearing   her name as a costume   as a gift   as   means of gathering witnesses
She carried it   like   well water   just above her head   all   the   way   from   its   source   to   its   seeker
Not   that   the   journey   itself   was   contaminated by   a   wayward   sun   ship
You   are   my   starship
You   are   my   tar   baby
Shut   up   stop mixing   it   with light

Far Beyond Hysteria

I guess I'm reluctant to write this shit

The one about the white hitman who coaxed me into his bed with some liberation fantasy

papers I couldn't read or wouldn't and left me for dead when it got too good

They took him to the madhouse to treat his fever Took me for a barn owl

and caught our offspring on a raggedy stack beside articulate livestock By Black Spring

we had Lena Horne and I was nearly a doctor to keep telling inklings and kindling

Crazy little me Beautiful me exuberant about my grief healing everybody but daylight

Headless Heroes

Then they started cutting the heads off of black corpses to keep us from suicide and it would have but then we saw the work cut our babies out of us like rain and running toward the strangled silence as glorious as rowdy as missing as proud as their jesus did Oh spurned shadow, don't you taste the crow

Maafa I already told you you ain't pastoral

Nor are you cidity though

Nor home

Nor anywhere else

Not that an elsewhere would be enough

Not that even shrugging is contaminated by ambition

here

32

Nostalgia is very legal   and   nothing like memory

Not   that I remember   when   I touch   a piece   of leather

How they skinned   her and licked the bones   an addiction

to   rescue   the disaster with no   name you'll   need some bodies

Tell me are you   some bodies?

Damn right I'm somebody

Laugh, Clown, Laugh

In a plush chair, the energy is flowing through you and its derelict shards and can be reduced part by part to terror so she sits you down. Restorative dreaming. In a dream you see what you've been busy ignoring so she lets you sleep in your terrible witness seat. In a television set you let the pleasure of images replace the need for action so your mother's body is dragged through the flood while you watch *A Different World*. Whitley lost in the hood during the L.A. riots episode. Simulacra and acres of precognitive magic shut into a laugh track to wag and waste. In a dream your tears aren't wet so you're actually awake pretending to be dreaming and looting in order to access a latent sense of yourself and your personal dilemma is you're just too happy in that seat, invaded by the kind of gratification that's really fear of the unknown. Don't feel bad black man in the big chair in the sky when they laugh and call your candid isolation music

Say music like it's a sickness here a terminal thing

In Praise of New Beginnings

It felt nice to be close and some days chained together in the dark we conjured a paradise of right there and black skin   never wanted it to end   sensed that it had been some   hidden desire to be together to be inevitable   that got us on our backs saturated in   funk and daze   realizing more every day that we were happening to   what was happening to us   and taking solace in that   subtle revenge as it accumulates   and some days savoring that pathetic closeness   giving in to the pleasure of touch blaming ourselves   and   allowing our nightmare to become our fantasy   and that was dangerous so we are dangerous   because it takes a divine soul to survive her fantasies to come out seeking nightmares beating her chest in a rush of justice knowing that the fool is the most powerful in the deck   the empress second   and   when you're both   watch out for   hybrids who are both and one and chained together on   this boat

we on a boat we are so close so in love   I trusted the body chained to me as my own   I trusted the danger as our power   and I ran away as you saw me there I was gone

Today my lover is trapped in a machine   I try rescuing him   but he's been drugged and is drunk he flails at the screen like   Damon Wayans and   John Wayne   keeps unfastening his belt My friends   every one of them   trapped in a machine drugged and drunk   the engine slapping them with adrenaline so often they seem to like it like to fake it   like an addiction and human touch the delicate swiping along a sea of dumb faces and tenderness and some mimeograph and some patterned movement in his wrist   to the sight of my throbbing picture

Our bodies made to touch   tucked into ships   became a network of delirious ideas rubbing on our throats like cold salt   held on to by secret fists of remedy   Maa fa   don't leave me longing for the sharp blue screen of sea   don't end in America   broken enough to be satisfied there   hold us side by side together the sun is just rising into a willfully vacant smile   the road is so vacant also it aches and moans for us to walk it   the high pure purple perverse incredible   the cliff I'm stepping over before I'm pushed holding your good hand as we arrow into the ocean giggling like nigga dolphins

Man, God Ain't Like That

And compassion forced to insert itself into moments of mutual suffering and lurk and crack you open
and taste and ruin the nasty opera of your wishes So now you wanna live now you wanna be
loved instead of worshipped now you wanna wear protective styles now you wanna fold your
eyes across mine like some minor kaleidoscope and think Ima not swerve or otherwise deliver no
mercy now you wanna love me even if it kills you wanna do me like you did white jesus and then
pray to me like Ima even cuddle or rustle keys now you want me to teach you how to live forever
or at least how to dance in a finite expression of something other than regret and you think Ima
not swerve It was the end of western thought we had reached its paddled cliff
fought our ways back to the restrictions of innocence so our virgin could sit on a vision and fuck
her boyfriend while his wife was at the party looking around like she was lost or had lost
something the cross or the crossroads or her Bone Thugs melody that was a hymnal that was a
double breasted jacket on Malcolm Little type switch in the pattern of loveless riddlers drifting
into car radios and infomercials in tears and handcuffs

Ma Leaving

When the disasters leave   the   house   and   you   feel   abandoned   betrayed   braided up, tho

Rows and rows of you   tamefro

 Let's   stick   to the evil   that   we know.   Repeat *when blood*   *was shed*   *love was gained*

She sings and his body's reassembling   she   sings   and the lock on   the chains   starts turning   the
squall of a rock in the heart   cracking   up through the throatback

Ma's Restorative Gasping

Had to clock him and run, tuff. But somehow in the photograph I was the one with black eyes. Now I understand the meaning of childhood. And the difference between compassion and imagination. When I think of that girl, me, she vanquishes everyone and feels no pain. I cannot imagine pain toward her, only the dance of it, the soft wince, the body making its muted mouth shape and then limp retaliation before regenerative collapse. But when I lend her compassion, the same girl, I see the bloody grill and black eyes blooming smudged purple as she swings at the monsters of paradise, amethyst knuckles, brash smile, laughing at them for being as stiff as minute hands in the hour of parting, teasing them for feeling valid in their former dominance, *whatchu thought this was*, loving them for their impotence without it, the machine I mean, the state, she struts to their broken fate in naked lace and suede, *just cause I don't eat it, doesn't mean I won't kill it if it steps to me rough and wilting* adorn its resting place in the stage of poplar from which we became so popular tree slur for turning new colors into sorrel and song and counting the days by how large a batch we made from light to light I swung like xanax landed on the eighth note of tomorrow: time travel as easy as doing what you came to do when you came to do it which is always *now* and I am very harrowing now and then I was bleeding and dressing my killer's wounds for a very long time Maafa was doomed by the same love that's saving her now

38

and finding begets needing even though we don't want you no more. That night we listened to Al Green together and pretended Berkeley was the Savoy and gave up soy and gave up rhetoric and gave up Rome and gave up noses and just laughed as the smoke dripped from our hair with the histrionic intensity of their branding irons

The alienation of labor is almost complete.

The shadow we wished to become is gone now   and the farmers listed as murders are turning   up
alive   in its place   *If you reshape desire you will reshape the earth*   they whisper   hitting
it with the hoe's edge   frozen in their deepest moment of provocation   and okay with it   their
bodies hoeing together   making a maze of guitars   the strings and cables   and Billy Harper   and
asking   like it's admit-it-or-be-cursed   and   forced into another labor camp, what did you make today,
show me ?   I used to think pimps were evil and lazy. I used to believe the white shade   was shedding me
in moments of   relief   and   exile   we stuffed needles in the blank and I saw my   ranking in the
compliance   my way of confusing dread with yearning   my love of looms with my love   of workers
(cld say *empire* in the place of workers, I love her mind, it turns like jacks on asphalt)   turning into   a desire to
possess some earth   to herd some sun   to exchange some light for   salvation   and what   was
that?   A   sweeter   kind   of labor   a rebirth   we deferred everything   and it isn't working

we are the first   fascists

Not that we are the first fascists
Having made ourselves up
of acrylic mazes   between the notes   and Winona Ryder
Wyatt Earp
Gambler, rebirth

The poisonous over-sincerity of non-sinners made me lead with crime. I mean, giving it all away, swallowing it all, they became the greedy heathens they shook fingers at and I wanted to meet some thieves, killers, real ugly beauty and leaders. I wanted to meet some mothers who were also whores and queens and Mary, why do you look so worried? The creaseless sea will carry me the evil-seeking was a trick about repentance I'd be rounding up the broken souls and lending them to the afterlife it's holy over there it's twelve endless hours between nightfall and a row of larks yardbirds I wanted Charlie to be black country and unappeasable too I got into the hold with no I.D.

The Damned/Don't Cry

As she was loaded into cargo with the others, still chained to his now faintly rotting flesh, they loosed him, tossed him into shallow ocean as if he had been a coin or knot of soaking weeds. Ma ah fah pretended not to notice, cried to herself privately, and then in the twenty two days it took to get off that ship, she forgot about it, blocked it out. Maafa is immortal, one among many girls who sacrificed their fathers to save them from slavers and was given the power to live forever on the boat that circles the sun forever. She is the god of massacre and no surrender, and the shabby nihilisms of any instant. This is what it's like for the god of genocide, massacre, no surrendor, total Sunday, this is what it's like to love her and be her

Not that John Cage sits on stage in silence but that Herbie Hancock sits on stage in silence

Not that I have re-read *Death of a Salesman* looking for him in the pulpy indifference

Not that I have killed you again tomorrow morning, to be sure

Not that I have turned anger into adoration with the sending heel of a lazy shank

Not that you thanked me and think me to life

Not that I was sulking in silk and echo

What   about   a   bath   of   light   on   the   letting

What   about   the   way   we   ruin   everything   is   peaceful   &   generous

Yeah! / Compulsion to Inherit the Wind

Remember enthusiasm   spasms of it so violent   like illness   waking up to catch his ashes   and
spit   the   grits   to   tune   the   drifted   moan   I'm enjoying this, this is crazy

Black Anguish

I'm not asking you to play Cleopatra and Liberace   that act is too bulky and very cynical worldly
people might even think you're joking or lift   up your armor looking for armor and find it
along with some bullet dimples   I just love   what a mouth does in rain   his face after the
arraignment   his wrists after the   shackles so soft   so   bloated and edemic roadless blue eroding
and   the baby crawling across   the alphabet   we made that   from the center of the trap we built
this life

It's just way more eloquent than anything to let yourself smile about it   The market would call
your enjoyment meaningless   all these captains of industry are thieves!   And today we took a
walk and laughed   erratically at the damp lenient scene, the chemtrails huddled   like rainbows,
hugging,   posing vibrantly for conspiracists   rubbing the sky with   their swiftness of filth   He asked me
why   isn't   that   water beneath us moving?   And we laughed all over again, heavier, more sorrowful.
It's   a toxic   waste dump   all the sludge is   rooting it down like anchors and husbands, I explained,
and   we kept laughing   uncontrollably now   and the rain sounds steal drums as us   forgetting
to act stolen

Duat

So   we   write   *black laughter*   and   the   word   slaughter   has   no   refuge

Lost slur   lost count   of   how   many   of   her

She   really   cracked   her   ribs   to   give   us   *Precious Lord*

life is   humiliating

We were still laughing

Not   the hero   but   the   myth   of   the   hero   slaughtered   no   refuge   for   her

Not   the   deadbeat   but   the   reaching   kleptomania of   every   living debutante

Not   the   revving   of   the engine   but the   the way   it slips   into   steadiness   when she's sunned

Tastes of   swamp   and palpitations   and   peaches   so   fuzzy   so   fussy   so   neat

A   dozen   representations of   harps   in   stones

If you feel like   you're going crazy   or   dying or   your   ego   is   dissolving   go with it   don't fight it

if you fight it   you'll   make it worse

My negroes, I say they are mine because my father gave them to me   the story begins

46

Humiliating   to be given so much   and trade it   all for a sharecropper daughter story

Dark bellied underworld   struggling   to reach hell   and name it after a laughing

Disaster   struggling for attention   not a riot or   a ruins but a paradise of ruins

Escape Scene

How I   chopped   the   gris gris   into   whistles   and   woke   the   whole   ship   to   dance   his   ghost
to   Alice's   tambourines   their   manic   softening   shuffling

I   fought   because   otherwise   I'd   be   mothering   another   one   another   one   then   paused   to
Soft   Machine   to   sip   some   dumb   iron   messianic   sap   and   a paddle   slapping   the   water   like   toll
on   that   ass   hypnotized   mesmorized   confidential   offering everything except myself

Leaving Duat/Got Til it's Gone

I spotted these floating prayers in the territory of pantomime
impersonations   of the nerve of a lion
And rebellion time, packaged as performance before it even
lifts the sun   was never one of them

Any remnant could be the serpent could   be   the   burden   could   be   the   reimbursement   we
incur as   debt   our hurting victory could be   early   signs   of   freedom   or   why   she
crumbles   a bull's horns into   the   oatmeal   and   feeds it to   the boss'   children   halfway
between   doom   and   sun   you   have   to eat   every   visible   bone   every white thumb
every venerable   omen   has   to   enter   you   until   you're   foaming at   the heart   and could
be   the serpent   could   seize   the   morning   as   your blood singing   to the sky   could
tell an   honest   lie   about   how   beautiful   trying   is   could seed   the   tension   that
crests into   dawn   as busy as   rumor   as   ruined   as her   rogue boat which dropped the
fire it was   supposed to show up   She shows up   abandoned to flames in   the distant drone of many
refrains

I wanna ride   tonight
I wanna ride   tonight
I want the Mothership to land right in here
And when it comes I wanna ride

Leitmotif (*Run*)

My Danger as Her

Handlers   lurk   for   saints   such   scams

And I became a saint when I was   seven   what   plans we have!

         Revolution   feather   pillows   foam   ones   former   slavers   for lovers

Resurrection cuddle   here   and   there   and   here   again   for salt   all infinite

   in   the trickling   water   a   tall   luxurious   gentleman   who is always nervous

about   his   card   trick   always   sticking   clubs   in   the   bushes   this paranoia

other   than   being   vain   and   homely   at   the   same   critical   moment of   disaffinity

     makes   it   easy   to   sneak   up   on   him   with   analgesic   soothe   ask rude nurturing

questions   nurse   his   addiction to   himself   and   run out   naked   into   the   throat   of
night

To   tell on   him   I   fell   on   him

          you   know   I'm   Corintha   you   know I'm Maafa   you know you're trapped

in   a cloth   dark   empty   parking   lot   with   god   your   dealer   and   a lot   of
                                                    sodom's moonlight

53

Maafa's Toneburst

Your vampires have clay feet   take this hammer
Your   cake has   mammies in it breaking form
To feed the   damned   your   dancer   rambles in falls
It's always so   full   wall to wall   wooly and Willy
All the thick sleepers   impersonating salesmen
for her   attention   and   then   atonesome   phony temptation
Plantation   tickles   cause it's a   quill of crop on the cops
A winded bullet a lot of bullets   Kwame says   as
Naked terrorism butt/ass naked not a care in the clench
Then/then   beaten   with the switch of   quick feet   stutters me
Them and the clay   feet fat of blood   feet   cash only
In a cryptocurrent economy   by *cash* I mean blood
and black kidneys by *only* I mean if you can hear me but cannot
count me   you owe me the town   and I don't need the town
The pawn shop full of harmonicas and car radios   the healers
And their hideous acres of pig shit in the air   I mean literally
As we eat the sky as their   feet chip adobe   photoshop fangs
Hot dogs come   at the cost of breathing   and the limpia does
nothing if the dung is heavy   ex slaves wheeze   of what it was
To pretend freedom could save us   from being traded for parts

I want to pivot to talk of gameshows now   contestants the animals
who left the farm alive how the phrase *let me out* grows wild
with lepers and purses   Oh, Lavar   leave it
How the angels have fallen   fallen

&

I promise to disappear   again

No Discernable Radical Politics, _Run_

Limping   such a tender bureaucrat
      Intent   on condescension   great at that but
Standing on a black woman's   neck   is   not   an   exorcism

  This is Eartha Kitt brittle and   exuberant   at the end of   compromise

Out of   sequence   out of gasps   out of   riddles   to   drill into   smoking apples   _Je m'appelle_   means
I   am   called and   I am called—

To seek   an   accurate   language   one   clicking   and   splitting   the tangled gulps   of   unmeaning
Numbing cream   lean satin glove on   a   cane   chain   chain chain   be careful—

The   calm   soul   chopping off a finger to collect insurance   money   for   her   eponymous
winter / _hiver_ see "vers" to go toward   the bees are   hovering   the   air   stings   in loaves
of   honey and showsteam   the   hard r hunting kit   is sold out on two-day shipping
to-day   slaves   and after all   that   you still lose faith   you're   still awful

patient   for footprints   on   Ma's skin   which   she irons herself visibly in   the trimmed
window   You're   so   funny   you look right in   and   smile while she irons high   skin

Pact

As   new   eyes   form   look for   me   their   envy   reminds me of graham crackers on rainy day care mornings   it's a flakey   pretentious   cinnamon   jealous of   the   thirst   it   causes   it reminds   me   who's lost and   where I   can find   my   father's finger   still   in   the barrel of his   .45

We   have   records   we   have   semi-automatics   we have   that much   and each other   Maafa for your love   the   musty seeds   of   Florida Man   munched to   smithereens for you love   they're never   buried   it   never rains on Venus   we never eat from boxes   Maafa   for   your   love a better world will blurt   itself   out   as   starmaps   and   archery   iron cast pots but   the   whole mouth is raw berries and rosemary for your love   Cinnamon makes us bleed   when we need to   it's a clean morning I   tuck   boss   in a   mudpack   beneath   a drooping thicket and   practice

his monologue back   at   him   limpness   that he is I   return in three days   to pick the gnats and worms from his muddy flesh and later add   them   to   the   cake and potatoes on his widow's   menu   They   skip no days of food for the dead   a miracle of evil   you   want   to taste impunity   so badly   you want to feel the consequence   of fake power in   your belly & I am very generous about teaching you how you want to feel   until   you don't want it anymore   beg away   your   desire   I'm not even angry I'm just very   generous   I   practice the boss' monologue   feast on   your   own   dead feast on   your   own   dead eat your own dead   and one   bright- necked   morning   you'll   see   a   rooster   and I'll be running no   more   game   on you   escape   is   blue   escape is   spring   lazy eggs

decorating   the new   likeness   the new   parallel hunt   with   relentless distance

Maafa Knows Benthos

The way the black bottom is all explicitly kiss my ass but our castaways have a way with nestle skeletal eel and urchin barren and the skulls of my friends of friends of friends sediment and merriment at the sea bottom sebum and press and left out too long jelly flesh of my flesh bone of my bone I am getting happy thinking about the long dead blacks straps of feeling in the marine era and reluctant to nudge me gently and giggle about a mineral trade come -up like these deafeningly cagey success stories they say digging up the eyes of the long dead and selling them to forever gets very low in the relay tomorrow they run like snakes and chase like holding a telephone in the pen hand snapping smiling my cbd finally came I'm playin been had that oil that skull road that calm knowing

Settlers, *Run*

Sadat was taken to shivering between shelves to get the gestures their geese and tell Jesus to eat nothing for as long as it takes to taste their coming color in tongue and ten ships and then situated like routine ruby mining or some electric time in the thoracic spent trying to discover your own killer I'm not a preacher or anything I'm not even righteous but I was there at the mistrial I saw christ crushed with a pestle of astral approach and fed indifferently as notes and nodding notches in this treescript the bark a cryptic parasitic fungus preparing synthetic adrenaline that has spun the feet into spasms so that each step feels like jumping hurrying an addiction to its invasive lift leaving before you've finished arriving and thinking it's cute to riot in new jeans and Egypt strut

                                                you   are   encouraging   ghosts   to   haunt

you   forever

And   ever

What an endeavor that longing was

What an ugly law to love

Maafa   save   us

Was it my fault   christ was   all   fake   at   the   altar

Was   it   my   waiting   fault

Ma's   Occasional Dancing Objects

One limb for each event   the   sentimental   globe   galvanizes   nowhere   man   who steps and hits and   rubs   and   wiggles

the   dictatorship   has   a knack   for radical   determinism   that   way it   won't   ever   be   too   late   to   slur   the   whimper   or   say dour and   mean   redolent of   how   when it   enters   flesh   the   branding iron   has   legs   and walks   the   stammering skin   into   submission   *Thembi*   and   embers   remember the   charts   of   flutes   delivered   to pacifists and   herders   who   use   them   to   laugh   a   little   fixed tilt   eradicate   Milton   for   someone   on   pills   and   parole   much   to   her   peril   she loves   the carceral   shape of   pharaohs   in   the   shoulder   is   a   lush   for   blushing   lacerations   that bubble   like   winded   flags   or   the   slow-motion   depression   bellies   There   were   so many depleted   ways   to   grow   Initial   this   scissors to the wrists   erotic   tickle   of sharp on tender   and   came   to   want   the   iron   as   a   trace   of   walking through   fire   or being   pulled   by   the ear   toward belief   in   the   power   and   delirium   of   scars*   as   they   disappear

*Scar of a star (Once a heart cell is damaged it's damaged forever. It doesn't replace itself with a heart cell, it replaces itself with a scar)

Who is you?

Stranded ravine   Who   is   making   the   greenbloods   fantasize   and   even   scout   the   culprits   of   our   own   sickness   Who is   leaning   on   us   this   much   whimsy of   emblem   Who   is   teaching   our   dread   its   feet

Genocide, Patricide, Ma's alive

Side by side on the brink is the safest place

Take my hand as mink collapses from my shoulders Brave Heart in there of the rabbit whose frozen blood stabs the others for never learning to hunt and feeding on the hunted is the only sin and you have eaten yourself alive innit wild to taste the lie that you are beguile the guard out of uniform wear his body to the skinning or be black in the hotel lobby together this evening They think I'm a sex worker the sweet whore in your war your Helen unpenetrated one come to watch you free the land

Maafa's Kef

Not that   there   are   roads   duats   broken   lotteries   and   a confetti   of   numbers   lunging   from his   eyes   come   to   realize

that   you stole   his   momentum   and   some   misery   alongside

What I'm saying is I love the acoustics of our ruin   god's   line

Not   that   I   am   fearful   of   rescue   *nice neck*   he   giggles   next

Not   that   my   several   goals   are   hazardous   I   look   up   at   his

Where   the   skin   slices   carbon   dates   iron   in   the   crates

Not that the   maker   is   falling   off

Chris   Marker   the   luxury   of   pauses   that trail   off   into   gusts

Not that I have tried to teach this war to dance   but these codes are locked in rhythm and   the
waves   love   to   swallow their scum   I   used   to   be   afraid   to swallow anything but blood
and grapes   and so   we   can heal   backwards   The   spiral   is   always   thorns   first
then rose   then   the delicate elbows to ribs it takes to remind us we get around
Then   they   lost   their   clown   then   I could   take   anything down

Where do you stay?

And   one   night   we   even   drove   around   with   dead   bodies   in   the   backseat   feigning   a   drive
by   shooting   don't   know   why   there   were   really   no   bodies   in   there   really   but   don't
you   ever   miss   somebody   on   the   road   so   much   you   make   the   ghosts   play   dead   play
dad   overdose   go   into   cardiac   arrest   on   savior's   day   and   get   ready   for   church   regular   sift
through   thickets   of   empathetic   deadones   to   find   the   hostility   of   this   very   dream   and   in
aligning   with   it   negate   it   become   the   reason   he   stays   Where   does   he   stay?

In   prison,   on   the   plantation,   Beverly   Hills,   somewhere   wholesome   somewhere   with
strands   of   sun   to   dismantle   the   pretense   of   closure   somewhere   with   open   heart   surgeons
somewhere   with   no   martyrs   In   summers   we   marched   and   squealed   about   how   many
hours   were   imitations   of   death   and   why   the   ship   that   carries   the   sun   is   sinking   and   who
is   brave   enough   to   tread   its   new grounds   No   one   was   brave   enough   the   paradise
we   say   we   love   is   dread   we   dread   the   paradise   we   say   we   love   we   dread
this   reunion   with   the   light   of   love   we   cured   our   dread   on the road   together

Maafa 22

Gentle clove smell   on the wind   high   above   the flamestruck ruins   let's wear muslin to the   candid
Dolphy   barefeet on sunfloor   dry heave   and as we   sink   deeper the reeds   vibrate into rivers
the   salt   eaters   die of satisfaction   not   thirst   and   the   fat of the   lamb   of my tender
mercy   is lenient/ sick with   parasites   on purpose so   when you   taste it and are invaded
and the   dazed saline traps   a fist   of   spider worms braided like the trite roots of baby   trees   He
tried to put a root on me   ended   up   the   thirsty dead   teasing and begging their   own enemies
for forms   and I felt   a   little   pleasure   *baptize me in this dress* I blurted   to shed
shore   with   wish shape   confession   charisma   and a pretty neck   If I say *let the skin*
take   me   in   the skin   takes   me in   If I say *who   isn't   a pilgrim   across   mute   distances*
the   runners   channel   the lisping stillness of Mozambique   in the   mouth   shouting bird
prayer   bird   of jade pray   *I heard that* Birdie Africa Day   If I say grab hands and pray
they   will grab   hands and pray   tuck the unopened bud into the   safe cheek   and burn   away
the   germ of warmth   and   worship

Maafa in Constant Gardens

I keep saying: to speak is to touch He says please touch yourself for me settles beneath the torch a middle c orchestra trying for seasons and to be about it Row of tawny orphan clouds spilling into new sky like the crackles in black school hallways after bells and the one come from the killers to swallow torches is talkative as a reach of sunflower pollen in the isle pollen in the limbic shyness of voices that can feel themselves copulating in the field helplessly like echos and cold moondust falling flinging itself at the equinox of broken crops that kiss to hunt the rain that suck on garnet to keep its charm away that chase the firefly into the beetle's name so you'll never know shit from magic unless you burn one down Oh cowards! How I treat your effigies like flags of unborn nations and your flowers the first fascists again fascism has a pact with spring &

Vicious Nonchalance

No matter how far gone he is   he   never   lets himself   get   killed   in   a   dream   and   what's   trapped
inside   his   head   as madness laughing   comes   out catatonic   screams   we   need   to   deal   with
catatonia   some   more   the   entire   turbulence   of   the   digital   world   silent as a   blizzard as it
nears itself   dirty   as   thursday   jupiter   and   rage   day   to   grow   and spill   we need to
deal   with   idols   and   the sulking boundary   between   eyes   and   yes   we   need   to   see
inside of   the   genocide   to   its   heart   which   must   be   broken   wound   up   & dreaming
of its   own   murder   it   loves go   so   much   we   must   deal   with   culprit   but   who?

I   feel   strange   as   an   angel   telling   you   to   shape your mind   to   die   but   Leon   lost his
mind   waiting   for Maa fa to admit   she   knew   where   the body   was   and   float   through
to   the tucked   black   shoulders on the white foam-bones of water   I   half remember   him   being
awake when   they took him away in   chains and suede   It's   so   hard   to   say genocide   but
Maafa   comes   out riding   how   the   savior rides   with   the   endless middle ahhhh or ox   and the
yes / no   eyes   at the   end of suffering when it becomes   delirious &   trustworthy

69

Maafa 11

I had different inclinations then   untensed declensions   I said   hemorrhage but   meant   clemency   in the   spilling
Nothing   would   be   leaking   like   news   or   a   crease   turned   noose   nothing   would   lean   into
the   baffled   incline   of   should

Ravishments

Not that I   was   fugitive   from every role but this

like   genocide is   the   begining of civilization   and   I   come from a generous madman

busy   at   takeoff   black   bars

                              black   eyes
                         catcher's mask
                         the rasp of the trigger
                         runner runner
                         where did your body go?
                          Bid on me, though
                       There he go again, another payment plan

How I survived   my   murder: gave it to daddy   and   Miss America   behaviorism   cherish   the
way I cuddle   the poloraid   and sway slow   give it June or a radiant April

              that's the best blasphemy, the best place for me
     Exceeding   the gaze   the beautiful hostility of black   backstage   is next best
It's an   afterlife back there   where all excess is doomed access   to the morbid   backlash of
getting in

Dusk, Ma

and repair   dozes off into reaper   at   the starcross   not of   sorrow   or   the casual sterility of   angel genes   but of   a   charged   neverending

nod   on the needle of   how   he keeps   running   faster   than   salt beams   with isolation   faster   than   the malted   situation

Still— she hates   the   tapered wobble   in the word   *daddy*   falls on   her   knees and   clasps some   shells   or   wristfish   a kind of   oceaning time telling   her   the   small narcissistic   difference   between   always   and   never   can be traced   like a   name   in your   arm   or   paternity   she is   the one following in   all   four   directions getting   him   together   in wounds of song   longing   to   name

all of these people helping her eat   the sky

72

Ma's Favorite

This foil Jesus meets Jimmy Baldwin succulent leadership   miscellaneous   neatness   neatness   in   its   nest of wicks   at this   altar   neatness charred   to   surge   Jimmy   at its   altar   & a   softer   less histrionic Maafa   cares less about   the   past but that doesn't   erase   her   shadow   glaze   her   baby bravery her hunger for its flesh source   grown   to   the   gated   reverberations   of   this   faint   humming beneath drums

She   was the subtractingest one   took   away   all   the meta graphine   metrographic   dumb   and left you with one   choice   one   ready   gesture to burst   into   confession   Aunt Hester   Aunt Ester anyone   but the holocaust's   daughter   tiptoeing   off   her   close   edge   closer   Fenty Beauty ambassador   hush money   laughing   and   blushing   lace

                    Not   that we've taken to   struggle   sheen   to hugging the glow of aching

Not that I'm telling you
 I'm not   going

A melodic name for a recurring human situation

And there you   are   all strung out   and all you've got is your little self

Not only that

He repeats slowly   on the verge of reprieve one last   spark of blame   adamant and remote

I want to go   up   to   the podium   and scratch billfolds slowly   so close to the mic your nerves tighten

And the joke   strangles everyone commerce hasn't   She   reaches   the most   comfortable armageddon

city with   a satin embrace   catches it imitating her speech patterns   and   starts pretending

muteness   not   only   that   all of her insight   quiets to   listen   to the pretense   skew into habit

Not only that   they didn't give us any land   at   the   reverse abduction   Maafa just stumbling
from place to place begging to be   enslaved   Not only that   she found   taker after taker

   Take her off my heart   her fingers are tucked in my heart petaling pedaling   everything
charged   and static   in

74

the flatness of   running   away   the stray monotony   of   it   how lonely   the road

made it thrilling to be trapped   in some   contrived   need   she   pumps in my knees   too a faint bruising beat   and beautiful   idea   Maafa   run   and   idle   come some other spring

Maafa's Waist-Length

Now   time   circles in   switchblades   in   jars   it   injures   believers

Fathers   are   about   to   be   obsolete   for   her

Her   luck   is   coming   in   to   shore   naked   over   and   over   and   over   again

Covered   in the   blood   of   enemies   laughing   selling   her disastrously special   luck is selling

Held   together   by   expectation   and the   blurry   magnetism   of   the   killing floor   Maafa made it

to Skip James   that part   in   story   to   remind   us   that   wanting   nothing   is   the   first

evidence   of   the   healer's   hand   no tone   scar   of hunger

My   name   is   Maafa   and   I   spit   star   guts   at   the   craft   of   ease

I own everything   my   knees   are   in this   mud   stewing   it   to   charter   searching

For the   mineral   they   are   tender   circles   of   blame   give   our   creation story

The   range   of   a   jaded   braider   clapping   her   bounty   down

Militancy / Intimacy

He's doing push-ups on the   soil   but appears to be   flying   fending for the entrance air   crow by crow
dive   I love his strong arms   rumpled and pulled   to pulse by the bolted   outcome / costume limbs
cut like numbers   If he escapes   if he cuddles wonder   if he visualizes the coward into bitcoin or
whistles   he'll hold the horse in his arms and stroll   they'll trot off into the   water together
powder dumb   to where the sun   glimmers   and blinds   and he   sings   when   he   flies   a vicious
worksong nearness to crying   that song   about how

when   there   was   nothing   remaining   to   eat   on   the   tradewind   his   brother   went behind his back,
cut off his calf and cooked it over   an acid fire   and they fed   and made it to   where   the
storyteller flies low to earth   forever   like   nobody's slave   brother   like it's not heartbreak day
in the   quarters   like Maafa is   not   his   daughter   lost in the holocaust   they call her   eating its
flesh together

Not that I   have   fed   on   this   flying   genocidal   I said I hated loved   made it   my
prey   erasure   to   watch   the   work   elevated   hands   gripping   the   good   dirt   into   easy
living   *Living for you   is   easy living* The   genocide   was   expansive   we   ate   our   flesh   and   found   it
more   and   more   heroic   passed   down   little   inherited   sabbotage

Not   that   I   was   violently   inherited

But   that nothing has ever   existed   unless it's been ruined into proof   of life

It was so traumatic all over but it's all   over now
I'm feeling   like   myself
        I feel like coming up
Like a clean black subject

I watched the massacre of my   own   family   and kept

A notebook   yet

Bodiless plot thick as in damn she

To prove we'd been   ruined   and therefore existed   we were true stories

Louder   Edouard   Kamau   how   do we rinse the double burden of comparison and nigger   off
our mood?

There is no empire left   to scold to blame for the sodden hill we climb   looking   just to
look out over   see who all is there   and   someone's on their   way   to tell me the
part about how

Not   that   white   shame   is   permissible   in   this   sizzling   yard   sticks   and   s tones   may
Buckle   shoes   curly lace   socks   six   year   old   Maafa   swinging   swinging   swallowing wings

Twirling   paradigm piece   scheme   this   terrible   feeling   that   all   we   do is   tolerate each   other
To   get   over   that   this   endless   tolerance   is   rancid   and   drifting   into   europa

Not that I cannot   love   with   abandon
Not that I   court   recklessness   for   freedom

Not   that   I   can   stand   the   thought   of   domestication   I'd   do   almost   anything
Not   that   scoring   isn't   as   bleak   as   indifference

Not that I can   get   from   one   seed to   the   next   by   beating   this   ground

This horror is simply the foreground of a wonder   Heaven   later   slaving   here

Here's a myth that destroys that whole world   pretending to   be   an   offering

Not   that   Ma   is   flinging   buds   into   the   sac   a   couple of   paddles

Her   good   black   dress   and   his   skull   off   to   the   road

No one to   tell   but   Slim   down below   and Slim is limping

a snake in   a trance

The technique of accommodation has broken down

Allegiance   winks   the fray to shreds   and I wake up

A Paradise of Ruins

Not that we begged to be stolen or still mistake a killer for a chaperone

In the middle of my own demolition   with the same thing making me smile   causing my bleed out, this massive massacring building   house   of   style   and be still. *Intoxicate me with your smile.* See, every good thing dreams of poisoning itself into pleasure, why did we ever pretend virtue exists, much less liberation, much less neatness, togetherness, momentum and some misery. The heavens are in stitches. Skip them. Keep it. And your discount adidas the texture of stride piano. This parasitic, I meant, paradise made up of our style will impale us when we fall. We'll land on programmable memories, gifs, memes, emjambed with the natural world to make skeletal unfurling. And we'll rest there in some terrible reunion we asked for and begged for and screamed for— when we reach it   it will be as reaching silence, speechless in the shelter of our gimmick filth as we watch it go by, go east, escape us, make us rich, make us speechless, give us locations   elocution   in a loop

You   repent too   much   &
Pray like   beggar
Pray like   a dancer   instead

Becoming the   element you're calling in and then rejecting it with   silence   which is its own kind of motion
The self lassoed with swell turning to sweat shivering in   the desert *that's not how I remember it*

There you go again even begging   your memory to behave   like   a promise

Even breaking   that

Locked in a song   with   no pliers   but niggas   yes   this is the paradise   of biggers
and braggers   and   r u i n s   never snagged   on ballads   or   suction   lids   that   pop skulls off
like dreidels   Do you know   anyone   on the ground?   When they play your music they are
hunting   you   down   and   the   more   flattered you become   the more captive   that deepening
affinity   is   exactly   like   liberty   so   that they can   attract it from   you   and drain you
of it   Who are they?   Graveyards and hard listeners?   Ours and sources? This obsession with
sources   is   another   pathology.

Don't you see
(lost at sea)
Don't you see?

84

There are things we say for style   and beat that   we'll regret for real

About the girl with the firearm in the background

Do you think you can rule the world on a bluff—

Be ominous with me for a moment. Be omniscient in the music with me

Grieving the decency   that feeble decency

Blockbuster slave movie

Trauma sells better than sex   but slavery sells best &

Genocide is always organized   usually by the   state

So my slaves eat Wheaties

Everything worthwhile is improvising

A Tangle of Pathology

Molly   lovechild   and   Ima   leave   Middleman   got together   traded

vetements & genders   but Moesha's brother is still missing   even

        the fictions   are dysfunctional   so what do you mean   flesh of my flesh

It's too messy   to love Eric Dolphy as his head splits open on the operating table

and Uncle Charles   falls out   with   the critics for pimping   like his bitches begged him to

Sell me. No, me scooting hints, leaning in to   finititude   for strings   (soul dance)

And he was so great at it   he wept for the lady   while slanging her   it   was a dream

As in   something   you wake up from   muttering

Girl, you look pretty.   Can you sing?

Let's never   get   free   I   love you   fuck you   Are we   recording ?

86

Because the exasperated beauty of Pharaoh's sound is really   none of your business

On this raft with a blunt in the eye of a hurricane it's really none of your business

Heaping on another dramatically brocaded velvet smoking jacket

Yanking the shoulder pads out with   your teeth   *kiss me*   *make the sound you make*

on the brass *in* *my* *mouth*   crawl into a song when you leave

And don't say   which one   it's none of my business but I'll be seeing you

In   that soft stunt of aroundness   curved and bound   imbricated

Make it look like skin   aspirin thin whimper   no more sinners here

A new force in the modern world   &

Lucky no law says you have to stumble into their ways   and get ambushed

black   music   is   the   music   of   forensics

 all my   dead   friends   come   to   me   as   songs

so   that   I   travel to   the   center   of   myself

And dig   the   last   pain out   with   the   shadow   of their   ghosting   screams

How wickedly   quaint   of the   dream   to exist as a heap of sounds only love can unlock

But at the time of the massacre   no one could count   the dead   with any accuracy

We had to   count   their   gestures

Neon letters flickering like bad eyes   ripped chattel of   strategic music dimming to slow the mouth around
the idea   of   word   or   name   freight of   wombs   moody groomers

We used to call her the sweetheart but she's still the sweetheart
    of the blues

Why can't they go back, stop the massacre   before it starts

befuddled at   having features   things to eat   &   futures   things to cross   over &   fathers   I   told you   I don't trust father   figures   distressed assets   why the   gods   are   falling   & are so full of rot it energizes   them

Rekindling our love of empire   where

Everyone   weird enough   to be   a savior   will be taken to the market and   sold with the sugar and gear

When   you   look   at   it   this   way   isolation is   worthless   and   black song   a straightjacket   we   all   wanna   ride   on   behalf of   daddy   is   this   genocide?   And if the song just   stops   in the belly of me   and   you   are   reborn   am I   just   reviving   my own hunger for violent   revenge   in   sound ?   The new moaners   take a lighter   approach   their cries don't grind   they leverage   push clouds   around   soft food   geomantic   as if survival is intrusive   nobody   screams   everybody's   dead   & I head   for the South and yesterday   while the cysts in the language still pretend   to be drums

Then the music sounded nauseous   &   I   was   mad at Mississippi

   A   squirm   in the   water   made   the songs   sick   and elvis

My dad could do   that   better than he did   a more natural pressure on his chords

and ridges   And   beat   us   too   & be back at rehearsal

for sound   check   unchecked adoration   while we black and blue dinner

Not to mention   all   the   ones who fake their deaths   again but there's

a lot of them   and   I   enjoy   that   category   of weary   and   eager

Haunting and   disappearing   You can always sense   when a dead man

is   still   using   words   on earth   you can hear him humming   his   least majestic urges

practicing what he might ask   if you knew

He was right   there   drowning in his own blood   over and over

He'd whisper *couldn't you   let life be beautiful ?* Or

90

Here is a southern gothic tale that's true

Maybe   it   is   time   to   devour   one   another   this   grandiose   sharing   could   be   the   new   commerce

The brainwave patterns of 40 subjects were officially coded with spoken words and silent thoughts

A violent indoctrination we placated to learn to read

What a boring patience   the one for   freedom

Here is Jimmy Baldwin in his apron greasing a pan   some   landline   intervenes   an endlessly   ringing   earth   revelations   (I been 'buked and

The other side of heartbreak is not ambition

   crimson gauze   wrapped in   god's   suicide

Some genocide is god's   suicide   adjacent and remote   a   gory form of favoritism

Shot 44 times   in the head   they   announce   readily   I will not   dream   only of security and safety

& he's never planning to be a minister   in this version   just gestures   of church   and grease

so duress   so wreckage   so woodshed bound in   skeletal   minstrel   so   rope   around the   season skit   when   Maafa   catch up with   season of   the   witch

   we   made the calamity   famous   endless

91

because it is not (yet) sublimated   rage

His   craven childhood   a rubric for   the silly hope   we all hide in our   skin   buckets   of
candy   &   the sweetness never   expires but its sucre fades   to the faint funk   of   daylight   in
a B   movie

The bad   deed of having fake   anatomy   links   cabaret   to   a brightly lit machine

And it occurs   to me   these ruins   are the   blighted heave of an   undone trance and   we
might   even   love   them &   ourselves

Again

a   mass   of   habit-tensed   muscle unfolding   into   the   archive of vengeance

a   delicate   jest   inside of   which   sharing became my coherence

We are atonal here   and combed out   god's dialog   so   glad

In disaster's sigh   byebye   Tomorrow dies of longing   and we go right on walking
Self-hypnotizing

        No one ever told you how much you can heal in one day

Is it too solicitous?

Is effective to make such   beautiful sounds   or affect   infected with such beautiful sounds

Is it the herd instinct   that makes words   go round   worlds   downed   like   poison

I heard most people don't experience   catastrophic   violence

Pity them   watch Fletcher   Henderson   do   a   time step   He's so lightskinned

   Has a Hitler mustache   speck of babble in the stillness of him   feet pattering like a police baton

Not that it's bad   to vaguely   resemble   your   very own   enemies

All of life is   predicated   on a certain degree of possession

Not that the ruins   are   in   exile   from themselves   for   resembling their enemies' fantasies

A   litany   a plan

Or   a floating tendon   useful for early   mystical initiation   a   slur or tie

Rich Homie Qwan or Buddy Guy   even Richie Havens   Where does an improvisation   begin   and fizzle

Like some   relations   or no relation at all

George Clinton is   crying in my arms

how   an altruistic   caution   has a hinge   on   him and he'll never get to be   maudlin   again

Lonnie Holley's   howling began then

Moralizing captivity   that viral riffing   he calls *high lonesomeness*

bipolar jonesing   *what if I rip your heart out*   and turn it into a supermarket

The ruins mention   that   we   were here   the demolition   mentions   our omission

The crackle of   fragments   Miles whispering   in my   ear   by the   pool

Monk spinning   his muteness   into   rule   visible   tyranny   of   good   sounding

Duke Ellington chartering   the mission of poise in his vocal   tone   accusing himself

Of everything   *play that again*   *look how   she   ate   that*   He collapses

Into   Maafa's annotated ruins   emotionalism and light   weapons   weapons made of light that invert
the   theft in   swarms   and mention   us   adjacent   data point warmth   Albert Ayler
dormancy

It's   the sleeping for me   his refusal of his own   sainthood at the club   and complaints

They be drinking   they don't really be listening   untranscribed   injustice   the welts   after beatings
and   performances   how   I used to be that devoted to   the pathos of masculinity

I'd let it speak for me or silence me   in grieving   overgiving

What they own of Maafa now is more complete in pieces   more of her speech more of her genetics

Not just her labor but her recovery from   overwork   the music of it   pastime pieces

Drifting   past paternity and   other meek fixations

You can see this mischief lift her spirits   and   drop them like baker's flour   to bleach and suffocate the
birch and its glyph

Indifference   addiction   trivial   in the nervous palms of neglected girls who buy their own hair every

Second   Wednesday   in   the dilapidated everyday

No bodies to   recover?

Black Ark

East St. Louis

Port Au Prince

Harlem

Watts

Newark

Detroit

You, boy

This your boy   Blueface

RAN AWAY!

FROM THE SUBSCRIBER. My Mulatto Boy,
GEORGE. Said George is 5 feet 8 inches in height, brown
curly Hair, dark coat. I will give $400 for him alive,
and the same sum for satisfactory proof that he has been
killed.
                                        WM. HARRIS.

Motown Records

Strata East

Black Forum

Strut

Buss down

You've been struck by

Leaving Las Vegas

Dilla's Basement

Treemonisha nem

Sudden irreverence   Reverend numb   Aretha's purses   full of cash

Some exposed midriffs   low level explosives   covert as business

Someday   somedayeye   I will wear

Hype Williams

Venus   by the time I get   his synthesizer   anesthetic

Breaking down   Mariah   I call yesterday

Misty Copeland
Katherine Dunham
Kyle Abraham   breaking down into   motion   to   the   witness

Federal Regulation 45 (they can sell live bodies but they can't sell dead ones)

Gif's fixed   apollos   transfixed apologies

Not that we made fans out of jealous detractors
Not that we made enemies out of philistines   on purpose
    looked like Phyllis Hyman   genocide undone and becoming

Maafa more often   Uncanny to be   other than   herself

She found out paranoia   was narcissism
She found out   both sides   were armed and dumb

Precipice   is   her updated addiction   everything she's   about   to discover once she   finally
escapes   not the act of escaping   with its brazen and buckled   sensations   but   the   idea of how
it might   feel   to become   more like   herself   What if she hates it   despises the lies of
the   *middle   class   the bourgeois   ally* and   prays   for another genocide   to get back in trouble

98

where she can recognize   something   that feels real   but this time let's call   the b-side
revolution *volition*   and that   massacre *sacrifice*   my   sacred   advice   Betty Carter's voice *this*
time   not   taking   no   chances   on   summer   romances   that   fade   in the fall   Genocide is

reliable   a way of placating   the needs   of   some girl   in   need of herself   &

unpopular regressions   like   bare   feet   on   raw   grain
as it pikes   through   the   dirt   begging   to   be   nourished   by   light   and pedal   flesh

Her survival   is   as dissolved   into these   isolations   of a lie   by joy   divisions
absurd   amputations   of context   for love

As in nobody recovers that love   of being   unnamed once called   Maafa   with no shame   and no rehabilitation

Cover your eyes   I cannot excise the genocidal girl from gnosis   or understand why I know this
Why   you're   standing by   like spectators trading   trembling images as the world dies   it's
dying of   YOU   killingfloor   that you   are   oppressively floral with grief/fawning

and all   Maafa   can do   is name   me   your imposition

Your Bluefacing girl Buss down   I   wanna   see you bussed in

To the   elite   district   or Granite City

the   clarity   after ruin   of demolition

From where   we skipped toward   our   little   emergency   like   a   star   who else is coming?

Who all is there?

At   the last   dream   queen's   scream

100

Do I go feral or farewell   clicking or   slitting   or   right toward

a dug up ambrosiaed blood of runaway so much   I'm   nowhere

Organs failing to a skit of lights as   we scream our way to fainting   feigning   numb   thing   all that pain

What a numb   and perfect thing   all mine   wondering   all the time

Why don't they love me enough to kill   me   or   maybe I'll make it beyond my fear of the good life

My dharma   my   best dilemma   some contrived belligerence I didn't know was honest

Not sorry   to that man   who   is just   a sound now faint or vague because far away

Their infatuation with Maafa will turn to resentment   as fast as she shows up   happy

Be late   spiral   be late   leave your head

The true   killing   is the contortion of the personality   into a set of learned reactions

Maafa   will   never   be   outraged again

It's going to feel like dying

Porgy

That's   a lie   she's angry again tomorrow   scribbling curses on loud parchment

Wearing Prince's look   of disapproval   or is it evaluation   ecstatic shade   shun them, baby

Ten Dollars Reward
RAN away, on Saturday evening last,
a small sized Mulatto Wench, by the
name of GIN, about 23 years old. She took
with her a variety of clothing, among which
were 3 calico gowns, one pink, one blue and
one yellow Nelson's wave. It is supposed
she was enticed away by a black fellow by
the name of DICK, a notorious thief. The
above reward, and all reasonable charges,
will be paid by the Subscriber, to any per-
son who will return the said Wench to his
house, at the first gate from Albany on the
Schenectady Turnpike Road, or secure
her in any gaol, so that her master can get
her again.   ROBERT M'CLALLEN.
September 15, 1807.   72ep

We've come so far   recovery could end us now   getting   what we had before   back I mean— that could be lethal   We   giggle   murderously   and thank every thief   curtsy to each   in near evil deference   This is a love   scene   trapped behind   a   slow singing massacre   of her own family there were no bodies to recover   recovery so lethal   of   a singer so   remote she narrates   the edge of   consciousness   percussive blueing   that unexpectedly   shifts   to the delight of ruin   delicate   collapse   pass me   your lips   unrecoverable speaker   of a no name disaster

Her   laughter that tangled   whip   that   trips us   into other worlds

103

The final stage of liberation   is   to cancel   Maafa self-immolation discredit the girl   preemptively find all of her prior transgressions and   broadcast them   one by one   until   you   become   the ruins   Maafa escapes through   that   immaculate condemnation   that   leaves you   without antagonists   alone in the disaster black magic woman

Where I've been   waiting   all my life   for dad to   get   home

And   he's   still   not   home   yet

Now I'm   ruining pain's   reputation   with   the   pleasure   of   acceptance

Addicted to the origin story I recreated   treachery and   abandonments   that would mimic   it from   dusk to dawn I saved the day everyday my duat   my savior way   stole   your   father   stole   your   husband   went silent   demanded privacy   in my paradise of ruin   demanded   the dignity of   real black chaos

Revolution is   outdated   we need a new   abolition   of privacy   a new plan of escape

Not everybody will become a robot polisher   there will be new   vocations   new rage new range and cattllebrand   exile will grow mundane

Having witnessed the massacre of   my own   and it's not over   more bodies to recover let's reenact the part where   we break off   into getaway gestures   lumber   splintered footprints   sorrow   squinting with visored hands   crawling   on jagged   unanswerable   resignation

Not that   she was tricked   into   denying   their   own   holocaust

Not that I don't want it

I don't accept it

I refuse to witness   myself   remembering it   becoming it   entering it

Preface to a one volume   suicide   note   :   resurrection   orange floaties

I am   destroying   the   pain body's   reputation   with all these surrogates   and they're   scandalous

    enough to   distract me   from   having   become   *Maafa*

Having waited   to   get   home   all   my   life   waited to forget home   all my life

Having almost   made   it   every night

Something's   not   right

          there's   something   chemical about   the   spinning   plateau

Something Genevieve or   Chloe   where   Maafa   used   to   be   some   medicinal   nowhere

She did a bad thing on purpose and was censored canceled differentiated taken off the
air discredited her hurt by avenging it the destiny of all disasters forced into
hiding where they thrive regroup return to forever

Tender Disintegration

Maafa is endless this is endless and unrecoverable reconciliation and dispersion Enya and an opera appear
in the noise and bend me down and over to rumple and scam the negro intensity immortal
Her work is to confide in the crisis as if she is somebody alive forever it is her bleeding
forever it is part of me and until I called her I was so ashamed of martyrs of feeling
the aspect of him that was r e a dy to cross over as cowardice or betrayal or even uglier *hope*
She always comes up in the mirror you touch your reflection
as if the tension of it could cajole you past the glass and into Europe harassed
all the way through by the Caucasus Mountains and interdimensional demon pledges that don't make
sense unless that really is a knife against my neck and not an ascot or Cobble Hill

It gets beautiful expecting participation s h o w i n g up to the fall in the etching box as
fuzz and tears turquoise rubber smile a slow crime in a bathtub Is it a crime?

He just wanted to see something about power

Held her up like a limp prize you win in the ring somewhere for killing someone who loves you and
she was bobbing in a ring somewhere for killing off her characters one by one and leaving them in
commercials and brand deals sick joke fib, hoax Give me back to Mississippi and I'll unwind
the story Give me back to god like a drill in slow motion ripping back Christ's final nail to reveal
us in the unbuttoned heart with him in the gutter of him she got her burden a gardener

106

James Baldwin said confession is suicide   and then Maafa said suicide is our best collective
act   our   fascinated   eternity   our   web of country and river   and genome   aside/ slick &

    Maafa   grew   to love each rumor   trapping her   thoughts in *home*

                                        Not that this   was a place she could   get   to
But that she could forget   it   existed
Give the word for her   back
Suicide as   confession
Projection as   confession
A purifying ordeal
You must be born   to die
  The   revolution will not be this confusion of temperaments   (the living and the lifeless switching places in
spurts of outrage

So Maafa made   herself   up
Then blew herself up   to survive
                    Every now and then the humor is a knife   turning
                        Or   the   newest   fetish   object   a guillotine
                            The last black radical   neck   neck   sky
                            and   now I have this perfect life

RAN AWAY!

MAAʃA. *Maafa* is the only word we have in any language for why we have a diaspora. African holocaust. The black woman, about 400 years old, disappeared herself last spring. She brought with her a mulatto girl child who also belongs to me. The word slavery is used in Maafa's place and eliminates all that came before it— the journey to enslavement, the killings and suicides along the way, the endless running away still ongoing. If we erase that passage we are erased. Maafa vanished. I will give $700 for her and the child alive, a high price for this girl I bought at auction who is no doubt unruly and unfit for the labor for which she was acquired, bred, and kept. She may be in disguise as a singer or entertainer. She speaks French and English with equal facility and learned to write when she was supposed to be resting for her day work. She may use her intelligence to convince you she is a civilian and not a slave. Maafa is still my slave. Maafa is a great asset. Whomever will rescue her—

REWARD